Successful Adjuster's Playbook

The Secret Skills for Providing the Best Claims Experience

by
John Bachmann

Stanley Crew

Stanley Crew Publishing LLC on behalf of IA Path LLC

Dedication

This book is dedicated to the Bachmann clan.

To my wife, Kristin, and children, Hannah and Logan. They are always right there supporting me with all of my crazy ideas and ventures. Without their understanding and support, a project like this would never make it off the ground. We've had some crazy high-highs and some surprisingly low-lows. But through each and every turn along our journey, we have grown and strengthened as a family. I Love You.

And to my parents, John and Joyce. I still have not seen a work ethic that could even match theirs. Whether it was working 1 am to 9 am shift at the post office with countless days of overtime or 3 pm to 11 pm shift at the nursing home, they were always busting their butts, but in a way that my sister Jenelle and I always had someone at home or traveling to our practices and games.

But it wasn't just the hours.

When I worked at the post office with my dad, people spoke of him almost like a legend. He'd work his case in the corner and everyone knew that no matter what was on his plate or what the next truckload brought, "Johnny Nice" would get it done.

And for my mom, her compassion and care for her patients was unrivaled. Patients were her friends and family. Not "like her friends and family." They were her friends and family. I still remember her making special arrangements for a patient to visit our home to watch an all-important Bruins game because the nursing home didn't have the channel the game was going to be on. He had worked for the team and had connections to the players and staff, but it wasn't at one of their homes that he watched the game. It was our home.

Table of Contents

Foreword

John playfully refers to himself as an "insurance nerd." As a long-standing, self-proclaimed "claims nerd" myself, I would say that is quite an honored position to hold. As someone who has written several books on claims, including a claims cookbook, and has even gone so far as to create an entire musical CD on claims, I am proud to stand alongside John in his love for this business.

I first met John while teaching a customer service class for one of our clients in the Boston area well over a decade ago. Even then, as a claims file handler, John was laser focused on the customer, how they should be treated, and the goal of having them appreciate the care and service they received. John exhibited a deep understanding of what it meant to be a true claims professional, dedicated to the idea that we are here to help people.

Through the years our paths have crossed a few times at training sessions and conferences. Earlier this year I had the extreme pleasure of being interviewed by John on his podcast, and was once again impressed by John's insight into the customer experience.

In his new book, *Successful Adjuster's Playbook*, John does a great job expanding the idea of "Who is the Customer?" early on. Relying on many experiences with his own customers, coworkers and managers, he gives insightful examples of how his view of the customer extends beyond the policyholder.

Throughout the book John talks about his Big Three— Listening, Caring, and Empathy—and provides examples of both good and bad, so that the reader understands that he is speaking not only from experience, but from the heart. John's desire to help the claims professional be a better service provider is evident in every chapter.

The idea that empathy is essential to being a great claims professional is close to my heart. I firmly believe that empathy goes a long way in claims. John truly honors me by referencing one of my books where I talk about the importance of empathy. He does an excellent job of expanding upon it and relating it to a real-life experience when he says, "It's really about taking that twelfth claim of your day and still looking at it as if it were the first."

In later chapters where John makes it clear that, "Claims is not your only role," he goes beyond the technical aspects of claims to make a point about who we really are as claims professionals. He ties it up nicely near the end of the book by talking about something every claims person can relate to: managing stress.

This really is a "playbook" for anyone who wants to improve and be a successful customer provider. It is a wonderful read, full of helpful tips and lessons.

Take this book with you everywhere!

—Carl Van, ITP, President & CEO
International Insurance Institute, Inc.

Introduction

*"Get on your mark, get set
Ready or not here I come"*

—Little Texas, "My Love"

When I first set out to put my words on paper a lot of questions popped up.

Will anybody read a book about non-technical skills for insurance adjusters?

Does anybody care about a career in insurance, let alone in Claims?

What should it be called?

There are few insurance-specific books out there. Even fewer that are talking only about Claims. And dare I say, barely any Claims-specific books that are focused on interpersonal skills. I believe the lack of quality works in this area leaves a gap. So yes, I believe there are Claims professionals that are looking for a book like this.

Prior to May of 2017, I might have said there wasn't a huge crowd of people excited about careers in insurance. I just so happened to have received a LinkedIn connection request from someone pitching their book. This person must have had at least 15 designations with a complete alphabet soup after their name.

As luck would have it, I accepted that connection request from Tony Cañas and my relationship with the Insurance Nerds began. There were literally thousands of people interacting about their careers in insurance, although there weren't too many speaking from the Claims point of view. So that led to my first article with them...but I digress.

Any non-fiction work these days needs a subtitle to give the reader some additional context.

I was reading best-selling author Stephen Harvill's book *21 Secrets of Million Dollar Sellers"* when a passage grabbed me:

> Some of the behaviors and strategies you'll read about in this book will be new to you. Some may sound familiar. But none of this stuff is truly secret. That said, it turns out that the word "secret" sells books. So that's why this book, and the knowledge within, is called 21 Secrets.[1]

Steve is a fantastic guy and an absolute scholar, so there should be no doubt that I couldn't say it better than him!

You're going to be reading about concepts and skills that are going to seem simple. Almost too basic. There are no ground-breaking secrets and even some things you may find yourself saying, "Hey, John, no kidding!" Although you may think of how simple and basic things

---

[1] Stephen J. Harvill, *21 Secrets of Million Dollar Sellers,* (New York: Simon & Schuster, 2017), 15.

are in theory, they are extremely difficult to put into real-life practice.

These are skills that need to be developed and honed throughout a career. And we'll have to continue to work on them together.

And like Steve says, if throwing the word "secret" into the title helps sell a couple of books, why not?

Origin Story

"But I've got friends who love me
And they know just where I stand
It's all a part of me
And that's who I am"

—Jessica Andrews, "Who I Am"

The customer experience of insurance customers, and more specifically Claims customers, is an absolute passion of mine. But it wasn't always that way. The passion grew. It developed.

Like many of you reading this right now, I was one of those that "fell into insurance." Shocking I know, but Little Johnny wasn't running around the playground at Center School dreaming of a career in Claims. But I couldn't be prouder to be a part of this amazing community we call insurance.

So how did I get here?

Well, before Insurance I worked for a college women's basketball team and had aspirations of becoming an assistant coach as well as hosting a radio show. Hosting "John's Country Club" on the Voice FM91 was a thing for a short time, but coaching never materialized.

When the contract for the head coach for whom I worked was non-renewed, it basically meant that she and her staff had to think of other options for the next year. There was some soul searching on my part and one thing was readily apparent, a career in collegiate athletics does not equate to a stable career.

So there I was in my very early 20s with no paycheck, no benefits and really no direction.

I went back home and a friend of mine said I should sign on with a temp agency that was feeding jobs to a local insurance carrier.

Hell, I didn't care where I got placed at this point. I was looking for a paycheck to be able to afford beer money each weekend.

As luck would have it, I was placed at the local carrier as a payment processor in the First Party Medical unit of the Auto Claims department. The adjusters would do their thing investigating and evaluating the bills, then they would find their way to me so that I could key in the payment information. That's right, purely data entry. And not the most exciting data entry, either.

I was absolutely green when it came to insurance. I really didn't know the difference between a policy number and a claim number. We all start somewhere, right? I learned the nuts and bolts of adjusting by osmosis. Sitting in the department around the team, I started to pick up on the basics.

Luckily for me, I am a quick learner and a position was opening up. The manager sat me down and wanted to gauge my interest. I think back to this moment and it's an almost identical situation to a *Seinfeld* episode when Kramer was negotiating a settlement for his coffee burn. Except instead of the first offer being a year's supply of coffee, I heard the word "benefits" and my hand was out for the shake.

So now I'm an adjuster. And that was the trigger that set me down this path of being an Insurance Nerd. A Claims Guy. A Customer Experience Fanboy. Right!?

Wrong.

For the next couple of years, adjusting was still just a job. It wasn't a calling or even a career at this point. Remember, I still needed that paycheck every two weeks for my weekend allotment of beer.

All of that changed with one claim a couple of years into my career. It changed the moment I first called a woman who would change my life. This call, and the many more calls to her that followed, are the reason you're reading these words today.

I reached out to this woman to talk about a new claim I had just received and was going to help her through. Yep, she was depending on the same punk kid that was more worried about his weekend plans than the claim in front of him.

I knew from the claim description that this was a serious claim, but I was about to learn how serious it really was.

As we began speaking, she set the stage for me. She and her husband had borrowed their grown son's new exotic sports car for a little test drive to see what he just purchased. They went on a bit of a joy ride and her husband was pushing the limits of what was under the hood.

The railroad crossing they were approaching was closing fast. And the perfect storm of speed, steering wheel angle and elevation change resulted in a rollover accident.

She couldn't remember everything about the aftermath, but she did remember that when rescue workers were trying to extricate her from the car, being careful not to worsen her own very severe injuries, she became aware that her husband had passed away. Her last moments with her husband were eerily silent.

I was crying with her at my desk. But at that moment, I knew I was there to help her through this awful situation. Yes, I would help her like I helped all those people with the countless claims I had handled before, teaching her about what to expect from the claim process and how we'd handle medical bills and lost wages. But this time was different. I was helping another person navigate the worst moment of her life and I was doing this simply by being there for her, listening to what pain she was experiencing, and trying to grasp what she could possibly be feeling at that moment.

Our relationship did not end with that first call. I use the word relationship intentionally here, because that is truly what it was. I was there for her just like I would be there for a friend or loved one in a time of need. But she was also there for me. She helped me see what kind of impact I could truly have on other people's lives.

We spoke on a regular basis so I could check in on her and her healing process. Her severe injuries included fractures in her cervical spine that required the use of a halo. If you're not familiar with a halo, this is an external, steel structure that immobilizes the patient to help the healing process. To make sure it is secure and that there is no movement in the neck, the frame is screwed directly into the skull.

Despite an expectation from her doctor that she'd have to be in the halo for approximately six months, her six months came and went. She had to remain in the halo much longer. This wasn't the full extent of our conversations. Sure, we spoke about how the healing was progressing—or wasn't in her case. And we spoke about what we would do about her bills and lost wages. But that was only about 10% of our conversations.

We spoke about each other's lives. We spoke about our families. We spoke about our hobbies. You know, we had the type of conversations you'd have with a friend, a family member, or somebody you cared about.

She let me know that her family were avid campers and that the highlight of every year was their Columbus Day weekend camping trip. It's crazy. I'm typing this on a flight to an insurance conference in Las Vegas and I'm tearing up, because I can still hear her voice like she was telling me all of this for the first time. "John, I'm never going to go camping with my husband again."

I will never forget that claim or the conversations we had. I know I'm not the only one with a claim that impacted my life.

This claim and this woman changed my life forever. Since *that* time, I have been evolving into an Insurance Nerd, a Claims Guy, a Customer Experience Fanboy, and I hope you can take a thing or two from what I've learned throughout my career to help you find, strengthen or solidify your passion.

Who Is This Book For?

"Who's gonna give their heart and soul to get to me and you?"

—George Jones, "Who's Gonna Fill Their Shoes"

I thought it would be easy to describe the best audience for this book. Heck, I'd love to say that everybody would want to learn about the secrets to providing the best Claims experiences. But let's be real.

Even though I believe that Insurance is a career destination people should consider seeking out, I'm also realistic. Odds are that if you're reading this, you probably "fell into Insurance." And you know what? That's okay.

As I said earlier, I feel extremely lucky to have fallen into insurance. And my passion for it grew over the years. But this book isn't necessarily for someone that's head-over-heels for Insurance already.

So who would really benefit from putting all of these words together?

I would say, an early-career me. Yes, that's right. This book would have been perfect for John Bachmann in 2003. So I guess this is my version of Brad Paisley's "Letter to Me."

This book is for Claims adjusters that have just started their careers. They are going through a whirlwind of learning on the fly all while handling claims every day. But Claims and Insurance aren't their life.

Sure, they want to be successful, but striving to be a team leader, supervisor or manager isn't necessarily the ultimate goal. At least not yet.

It's my hope that this book not only helps new adjusters continue to develop a solid foundation for their careers, but also that it instills in them a passion for the work they do. I want to show that it's not just about inspecting, investigating, evaluating, and resolving claims. It's more than that. It's about helping people. It's about impacting their lives.

But this book isn't just for those early-career adjusters.

You might even be a pre-career adjuster. You are looking at different industries and noticed that insurance is an industry with lots of opportunities for stable careers. And a good starting point is in Claims.

You could be one of those students jumpstarting their career in field adjusting with Chris Stanley at IA Path. Chris and his team will help you with the technical aspects of adjusting, but this book will help with the human-to-human interactions.

And this doesn't have to be only for folks just starting in Claims. You might be a salty veteran. You've handled thousands of claims throughout your career. This book will help put things into perspective on a human level. The goal is to shift your mindset from moving from claim to claim to understanding that you are impacting another human's life.

If you're still reading this, that likely means you fit into one of these categories. Or you at least want to learn more. I'll stop here and say thank you. I really can't begin to show my appreciation and I'm excited to share with you some of the things I've learned along the way.

Before we can talk about the "hows" of proceeding with a successful career in Claims, we need to understand our customer.

Who really is the Customer when it comes to Claims?

Who Is The Customer?

"These are just a few questions I have"

—Clay Walker, "A Few Questions"

One thing you are going to learn about me is that everything we're going to talk about is directly related to customer experience.

I'm not alone in that.

Take a look at your company's core values, mission statement, vision statement, etc. I have no doubt that you will see something in there about Customer Experience, Customer Care, Customer Service, or at least something about the Customer.

If these aren't incorporated into everything at your company, there's a bigger problem we need to discuss!

A successful career in Claims is directly related to the experiences we give our customers.

So who exactly *is* the customer? How can we give these amazing experiences if we don't know who our customer is?

The obvious answer might be that the customer is the policyholder, also known as the insured.

OK, I'll give you that one.

But Claims folks deal with a number of different people on any given claim. Is the insured the only person that is our customer?

Of course not.

If I were to develop a mission statement for a Claims division, department, team, or even an individual adjuster, it would read something like this:

> To keep the promise of the insurance company that we will be there for people when they need us the most and to assist them through some of the toughest times of their lives in order to get them back to where they were before they suffered their loss

If you noticed, I didn't mention anything about "only people that give us money" or "people that signed a contract with us."

Rather than looking only to individuals that do something for us (i.e. pay us a premium) as customers, how about we flip the script?

What if we say that customers are any individuals that we can help?

So let me challenge you and say that we should view third party claimants as customers as well. Sure, they don't pay us a dime, and they certainly don't have a contract with us. But our purpose is still to help them through this difficult situation they've found themselves in with our insured.

Don't worry if you're struggling with this mindset. You're not alone. I didn't always see it this way. In fact, I probably was on the completely different end of the spectrum.

As a liability adjuster early in my career, I always saw the relationship with claimants as a battle. It was always a competition against the claimants themselves or their attorneys. A successful claim in my eyes was when I "won."

Now I can think back to the exact moment, the exact call, when I was challenged to change my mindset.

I was in my first few days as a liability adjuster in a Property unit. I was speaking with a claimant about her claim. The more we disagreed, the louder I got and the more I felt like I was impressing the other adjusters around me.

That's when I got a pop-up on my computer screen from my new manager:

"GET YOUR BUTT OVER HERE!"

Now I'm not sure if that was the exact quote. "Butt" may not have been the exact word and there may have been two or three more exclamation points that I failed to transcribe.

So I wrapped up the call, still feeling good about myself, because I was "winning" with this claimant. Since my new Property department usually dealt with policyholders, I figured I'd be all set once I explained to my manager that the person on the phone was "just a claimant."

The exchange went a little like this:

> "Hey Bob, no need to worry. She was just a claimant. We're all set."

> "John, We don't do that over here."

> "Yeah, I get that. But she was a claimant. It wasn't like she was an insured."

> "Like I said, we don't do that over here. I don't care who the hell you're speaking to. We respect everyone. You're here to take care of that person. And you're here to do what you can to help people."

Well, that didn't go as planned, now did it? Talk about a kick in the butt! But it was a kick in the butt I needed.

Claims in and of themselves are extremely stressful and emotional. People file claims because something bad just happened in their life.

Let's think about it from a claimant's perspective. The stress and emotion levels are ratcheted up big time. Not only are they now going through a tough time in their life, but they're also dealing with someone they never wanted to deal with.

They don't know much about you or your company or how well you may or may not treat your policy holders. So how can they go into a claim feeling good about how you *might* treat them? How can they trust us if they don't even know us?

This is why first calls and first impressions are so important. They're our opportunity to show them that we do care, that we do want to help them. They're our first opportunity to gain their trust. But only if we give them a reason to trust us.

The easiest way to begin is to be honest and authentic with them. If this is your first time speaking to a claimant, what's wrong with saying, "I know this is a very tough time for you, I get it. I want to make this process as simple as possible for you and hopefully I can take away some of your stress"?

Sure I'm going off on a claimant-is-our-customer tangent here. Keep in mind, our obligations are still to our policyholders and ensuring that we are their advocates. But giving a third party claimant a great experience is not contrary to this.

But let's not stop at policyholders and claimants. We serve other customers don't we? What about our insurance agents? What about our underwriting departments? What about our co-workers? If we're independent adjusters, isn't the in-house company adjuster our customer too?

I believe that what we are going to dive into for the rest of this book will serve to help us in all of our interactions, whether that interaction is with a policyholder, a claimant, an agent, an underwriter, or a company adjuster.

The Big Three of Claims Customer Experience

"It's a hard, hard lesson
But you're gonna have to learn it"

—Diamond Rio, "Nowhere Bound"

When I was growing up on the North Shore in Massachusetts, professional sports in Boston weren't what they have become over the last couple of decades. There was no Brady and Belichick. The Curse of the Bambino was alive and well. Jeremy Jacobs was more concerned about writing checks for his businesses in upstate New York than paying his skaters what they deserved.

But there were THE Big Three. And no, I'm not even going to give you the time of day if you bring up the other "Big Threes." There was only one. Bird, McHale, and Parish.

OK, I got my two cents in about growing up a homer sports fan in Boston. Back to the regularly scheduled insurance programming where I want to talk about another Big Three.

There's a Big Three that relates to customer experience in claims. These are not earth-shattering. They should be obvious. But putting them into practice is a completely different story.

Handling claims is not an easy thing to do. You are dealing with individuals who are going through some of the hardest times of their lives, even if in our minds, "we've seen worse." Plus, in these hard times, we are bombarded with negativity whether it's intentional or not.

I mean, let's get serious people.

The people we are interacting with are quite possibly having one of the worst days of their lives. We're speaking with them because something terrible happened to them, to a loved one or to one of their most valuable investments. I think it's fair to say that any of us, in their situation, might be acting in a way that may be a bit more negative than our "normal" selves.

And let's not forget about the never-ending pile of new claims, inspection appointments, telephone calls, emails, faxes, snail mail, etc., on our own desks. It can be easy just to go from task to task, policy to policy, and claim to claim without a second thought. Putting out fires (figuratively of course, even if you are on the property side) seems to be a regular occurrence. You can have the most well-intentioned plan in front of you, but something always seems to come up, whether that be an unexpected call, a new claim assignment, an email from an upset customer, etc., that prevents the plan from working.

So, although the Big Three I'm going to share may trigger a "well, yeah," from you, I can assure you it's not an easy task to put them into motion on every claim, every call, or every situation. But really, it is what we owe our customers.

Remember there is only one thing an insurance company sells. A promise. A promise that the Claims team will be there when the customer needs them most. When an awful situation involving what they value most occurs, the Claims team will be there to help them pick up the pieces and start to put them back together again.

We owe it to our customers to deliver on each of the Big Three skills on every interaction.

We need to LISTEN
We need to CARE
We   need   to   EMPATHIZE

You may have heard of these skills (or others like them) referred to as "soft skills." Claude Silver, the Chief Heart Officer of VaynerMedia, wants to stop using this phrase. The word "soft" is so belittling when referring to these skills. As we've already touched on, these skills are not easy to put into practice. If anything, these are the hardest of skills. We should give them the respect that they're owed. They're Hard Skills.

I was speaking about this topic just recently and a friend offered another option as well. Now I'm not sure if my Boston accent kicked in (*hahd* skills) and was misheard or if they were just flashing their genius at the moment, but they referred to them as "Heart Skills."

Hard or Heart both work for me. These are the foundational skills that are needed to ensure the best possible experience for our customers.

Listen

Anytime I start to talk about listening, my mind automatically goes back to *White Men Can't Jump*, when Sidney Deane is explaining to Billy Hoyle the difference between listening to and *hearing* Jimi Hendrix.

Now this discussion doesn't have to apply only to psychedelic rock. We can apply this to the claim experience as well.

We can just sit back and listen to the actual words that are being delivered to us. Or we can actively participate in the discussion in order to truly hear what the other person is saying. To know what they are experiencing. To better learn about them and their situation. If we do this well, our customers will give us the road map of how we can help *them*. Our customers will tell us exactly what they need, though maybe not directly. We need to let their voice help us to hear them so that we can in turn help them.

The way we can do this is through active listening. This is a process not of listening to prepare a response, but listening to actually hear the message that is being delivered. To get a better handle of the root cause of what the customer is feeling or thinking. And this will provide us with crucial information about how we can make the situation optimal in the eyes of that customer.

Active listening is not easy. Keeping your mind open and not formulating a response the entire time is not easy or natural. I, for one, have to remind myself, even multiple times in the same conversation, to stop. How often have you been in a conversation, you have the best line ready to go and you know just how to deliver it, and then you realize, "uh oh", you just missed the last few seconds of what they were saying? In those few seconds, you may have just missed the Holy Grail that makes the difference between a great experience or one that leaves the customer wishing for something better.

One way to combat drifting off to "Response Land" is to take notes. This is easiest for a desk adjuster as a majority of their interactions are over the phone where maintaining eye contact isn't required. Having said that, if you are meeting customers in the field, asking permission to jot down notes during the conversation will not only help you listen, but it will also show your respect for the customer and what they're saying.

Now I'm not looking for anybody to act like (or hire) a court reporter to get every word that is said. If anything, that will hurt your listening even more because you'll be more worried about what words you may have missed as opposed to what the person is saying. I jot down key words or phrases that will tell me what they're thinking or feeling, a specific pain point they've experienced or think they'll experience, or key considerations that may impact how the claim process may flow.

And be mindful that just because they've taken a breath or paused slightly, it does not mean it's your turn to start talking. So much information can come out of silence if you just let it be. Take an extra breath yourself. The Insurance Elephant himself, Pat Kelahan, keeps it simple for us. He recommends that we "ask...then shut up!" It's not always easy to do, but the silence that you leave can unlock so much valuable information.

When it seems clear that it's your turn, stop. It's still not your turn. We're going to dive in a little deeper. This is where your notes come in to help. Go back to one of those key terms or phrases and let it help you learn more.

This act of reiterating the customer's exact words back to them will do a couple of things. It will drive home their point and show that you heard what they were looking to accomplish. You're now on the same page.

The second thing that it does is that, if you missed their true point, they will correct you so that you do have it this time around.

You may dive in by asking questions like:

Now you mentioned that you had some experience with that body shop. How was the previous experience there? Was there anything you wish could have been done better?

Or:

You said that you have a vacation planned. Will we need to wrap up the next step before you leave so that you can just enjoy your trip or would you prefer to deal with it after you return?

Using the customer's own words when going through this recap exercise will also help bridge the communication gap. And a communication gap is usually the root cause of any claim that goes awry.

Care

There are a lot of reasons why people turn to a career in Claims. I've heard plenty of them, like the stability, the money and benefits, the ability to investigate different claim types and different scenarios.

But the reason I come across more and more each day, and why people start and stay in Claims is that they want to help people. At the very heart of it, that's what Claims really amounts to.

It's helping people get back to where they were before something went wrong in their world. To walk with those customers along the journey of being down and out and ultimately getting them back on their feet.

If we truly care about this mission, our mentality will shift away from being "open a claim, close a claim, move on to the next claim." You are the hero in a tragic story. You swoop in to help customers by saving the day.

Superman and Wonder Woman weren't in the mindset of "villain commits crime, stop the villain, move to the next villain." They cared about the mission they were on.

Listen, I've seen it in my own career and heard it from others. It's not always easy to care about every claim.

And I've even seen the progression of what a career in Claims is all about.

This progression starts out with a green adjuster. The adjuster doesn't know what they don't know. The first two or three years is a whirlwind of learning. Learning the job. Learning the policies. Learning how to interact with customers. Learning how to interact with vendors, attorneys, public adjusters, etc.

Next up, usually around years three through five, the adjuster thinks they've seen it all. And because of that, they become cynics. They believe every claim has an element of fraud. And they're out to get the bad guys!

Then, finally, comes the realization around year five when the adjuster thinks, "Maybe I haven't seen it all." They start having conversations with attorneys and public adjusters and realize, "Maybe they're not out to get me." They realize that they are still learning everyday and they see different claim scenarios they never thought they'd see before. Or they hear stories they've never heard before. Because they've given their time to listen and care about what is going on with that customer's life, they are suddenly open to growing again.

At this point, they often look back and think, "Wow, I really did help a lot of people. And I can keep helping people. I make a *huge* impact on people's lives!"

Sure, there are adjusters that don't ever progress all the way through. And I think it's sad that people get caught in a cynical mindset, thinking that everyone is out to get them and that the adjuster's job is to win.

But the adjusters who truly care and the companies that employ these adjusters, they can use this to their advantage. It is what separates the great adjusters from the rest, what separates the great Claims departments from the rest, and what separates the great insurance companies from the rest.

And it was no surprise when I was speaking with Claims leaders across the country when researching this book, that each and every one of them had *the* story: the one claim that touched them; the one claim that moved them; their "legacy" claim.

Whether it was:
- The Superstorm Sandy victim who spent on top of the refrigerator holding her children so they wouldn't be swept away by the ocean
- The claimant who thanked the adjuster for being there with her after her young child passed away
- The single mother who recently lost her husband, and was now dealing with wind damage to her home, alone
- The elderly woman with desperation on her face whose contractor failed to repair the previous damage which ultimately resulted in a subsequent claim

- The man who asked the adjuster to step into the barn to finish their conversation after berating the adjuster, only to have the man collapse in tears confiding that he had to stay strong in front of his family
- The man who texted the adjuster to wish him a Happy Thanksgiving and to just chat about the Dallas Cowboys many months after the adjuster resolved their water damage claim
- The woman who could not possibly go back to the property for the inspection because she lost her cats in that fire and who said even after the repairs are done, she may not be able to return

I can tell you each and every one of these stories for one reason. The person who was handling the claim cared. They cared about the people they were helping. Those customers made an impression on these folks' lives. They still vividly remember details 10, 20, or, in one case, even 37 years after the claim had been resolved. Yes, one of the people I spoke with knew exactly when they helped their customer through their claim.

What stood out is that during these conversations, a lot of the people didn't remember specific, technical details.

But they know exactly how they felt then. And they know how they feel now because of that claim.

Many had difficult times telling the story. Some became emotional. Others felt chills when bringing up the story. And most realized that because of the impact that claim had on them, their job was a lot greater than just the tasks.

Sure, at the time when they were going above and beyond for their customer it might not have seemed to be a big deal. They were just doing what was right in that situation. But many years later they look back and see that when people needed them, they cared enough to be there for them. And not just to cut a check for repairs or medical bills, but to be there for them, just like a friend or family member would be.

Customers will recognize this. They will feel it when an adjuster really cares during the claim process. And when they recognize this, they will stay customers longer. They will tell their friends and family about how those adjusters made them feel.

In Cleveland in 2018, my friend Ryan Hanley was giving a keynote at the Agency Nation Elevate Conference. He ended his keynote in classic Hanley fashion when digging in about this concept of caring. He said:

> Giving a sh*t is important. And if we focus on it, caring, not tactics, not strategy, not technology…but caring is our competitive advantage.

And you, the adjuster, can give yourself a distinct advantage the more you care about your customers. A key step to caring more is learning to empathize with your customers.

Empathize

Empathy has been a word that has been thrown around in our space for quite some time. It's almost getting to the point of becoming a buzzword. I hope we don't get to that point as empathy is so crucial for us to provide a great Claims experience.

So what exactly is empathy? What does it mean?

According to Dictionary.com empathy is

> the psychological identification with or vicarious experiencing of the feelings, thoughts, or attitudes of another.[2]

Got it...so what does that mean?

To me, it's truly understanding what the other party is feeling or thinking and meeting the emotional needs of that individual. And Carl Van, the author of *The 8 Characteristics of the Awesome Adjuster*, made it even easier to understand when he wrote, "Empathy is understanding where people are coming from; it is understanding that they have pain...it is simply understanding where the pain's coming from and that they have it."[3]

---

[2] Dictionary.com, s.v. "empathy (*n.*)," accessed August 18, 2021, *https://www.dictionary.com/browse/empathy*.

[3] Carl Van, *The 8 Characteristics of the Awesome Adjuster,* (self-pub., 2011), 119.

When I was chatting with Claims leader Alex Clay about this topic he wanted to stress a point about what empathy wasn't. Alex was explaining that being empathetic doesn't necessarily mean being a bleeding heart. And it certainly is not reading, "I'm so sorry to hear about your loss," from a call script.

He said adjusters should strive to humanize the entire process. To make a connection with the person they're working with.

When I asked Alex to expand further on this, he said to treat the people you're speaking or meeting with as if they were a friend. If a friend just had a water loss in their home, would your response be to say, "I'm so sorry to hear about your loss," and continue on with scripted questions?

Of course not.

You'd want to know how they're doing, how they're holding up, and how you might be able to help them. You may even utter the phrase, "If you need me, call me." This is what we should be striving for. To have a real, human conversation with our customers where we treat them as if they were a friend or part of our family.

When we do so, we'll get to a point of knowing what their true pains are and ultimately how we might help them through those pains.

During my conversation with Pat Kelahan, he went down this path as well. If you're meeting up with someone about their wind-damaged roof, empathy isn't, "Hey, I had a roof claim once too!" Just because that is the case, it doesn't mean you understand their specific situation and what they are going through emotionally. Trying to force yourself into this "common ground" may not be what this customer needs.

Let's get back to what empathy is. It's really about taking that twelfth claim of your day and still looking at it as if it were the first. Having a clear lens to look through to know where they are coming from, emotionally, during this time. And trying to think how we might think or react given the same circumstances.

This empathy might not be feeling bad for how they're feeling or for the damage. It may just be a connection that seems simple to us, but will go a long way for the customer. That twelfth claim of your day may be the twelfth hail damaged roof you've inspected. You've seen what the damage looks like on the previous eleven. You've even seen the size of the hail a number of times. But this twelfth customer saved a baseball-sized hailstone to show you and "help" you with the claim. She feels like she is doing her part and you should honor that. Show your appreciation for her help.

Empathy even encapsulates the way that you are communicating. Carl Van teaches that very slight variations in the way that we relay information can have an extreme impact on how our customers feel.

Take for example when we hear that a customer doesn't understand a process that we just explained or we notice that they have that deer-in-headlights look after saying something. We could say, "It sounds like you're confused," or we could say, "Let me explain this better for you." That minor shift takes the burden from the customer and puts it back on us, because we understand what they're feeling or thinking. The first example is putting the customer at fault. The second example shows that our goal is to help them.

In this day and age when we continue to hear about artificial intelligence, machine learning, self-service apps, drones, etc., and how these are a threat to human adjusters, we need to make empathy our differentiator. All of these technologies will take tasks off of an adjuster's plate, but ultimately they will allow that adjuster to focus on the human element and truly make connections with and impacts on our customers' lives. The human connection and the human-to-human interaction has not and will not be automated out of our line of work.

In a podcast "mash-up" of different speeches that Gary Vaynerchuk, Chairman of VaynerX and CEO of VaynerMedia, gave a few years back on *The Garyvee*

Audio Experience, Gary goes right into this topic saying:

> We are on the dawn of the era where emotional intelligence is about to become the single most important trade. That skills through technology growth will continue on a daily basis to be commoditized, but your emotional capabilities to interact with others will become [a] very, very important trade.[4]

As Gary points out, those technologies that we see in our space will be commoditized, however our ability to understand our customers will be critical to our success.

---

[4] Gary Vaynerchuk, "Firing Your Top Employee, Giving More Than You Take and Leaving Your Ego At The Door," *The Garyvee Audio Experience* (podcast), *https://podcasts.apple.com/us/podcast/the-garyvee-audio-experience/id928159684?i=1000433741295.*

The Vowels of The Ultimate Claims Experience

"Oh, who are the people in your neighborhood?
In your neighborhood?
In your neighborhood"
— The Cast of Sesame Street, "People in Your
Neighborhood"

Like some of you, many of my mornings growing up were spent in front of the TV being told that this latest episode was brought to me by a letter. Just like the lessons we learned from the big, yellow bird and his crew on that famous street, we don't have to over complicate things.

Over the next pages, we're going to take some powerful concepts and simplify them into a list based on our vowels.

Heck, we've already spoken about how tough it is to be an adjuster. Why would we make it even more complicated by putting together a system that is hard to understand or remember?

It's about simplifying. But keep in mind, like Stephen Harvill says, simplifying does not mean making it easier.

Similar to the Big Three, these concepts aren't going to be the most amazing revelations you'll ever read about, nor will they be super easy to put into practice. Rather, it's about building a consistent framework to put you in the best position possible to ensure a Customer Experience that your Claims customers will appreciate.

Although similar to the Big Three, we do have our differences here. Whereas the Big Three are the hard skills we talked about, these concepts start to move toward more tactical approaches.

One way to think about the differences is a concept that Gary Vaynerchuk refers to as "Religion versus Tactics." Gary wants folks to consider the deeper meaning and the mindset, A.K.A. the "religion", when looking at a process that needs to be improved rather than the tips and tricks, A.K.A. the "tactics."

That's why we start with the Big Three. We can use them to develop the "religion." The next few concepts, which I call "The Vowels", are the tactics that we'll use to drive home that optimal experience for our customers.

A - Anticipation

Over the course of a career in claims, an adjuster will handle thousands upon thousands of claims. As we touched on earlier, the sheer volume of claims could send us down a dangerous path of jumping from claim to claim without a second thought as we struggle to get through our caseload. The number of claims may seem like the biggest hindrance to providing an ultimate experience for your customer.

What if we look at things from a different angle?

Let's consider that each claim we handle is building upon our experience. This turns us into seasoned veterans for the kind of tricky situations we never thought we would encounter, but have now come across on multiple occasions.

It's as if we can almost predict what may happen next: the good, the bad, and the ugly.

This gives us a great advantage when we're helping to educate a customer. We can help them navigate potential hurdles and pitfalls long before these things even materialize.

Although we see these claims on a regular basis, statistics tell us that the odds are that the customer we're dealing with has not had a claim, ever. According to The Insurance Information Institute, only approximately 6.15% of policy holders filed a collision claim in 2017[5] and during this same year 6.26% of homeowners policy holders had a claim.[6]

Based on these stats, we can assume that the customer we're talking to likely has never experienced a situation like this before. Therefore, we have to provide a detailed road map so that the customer isn't surprised by any twists and turns along the road to a resolved claim.

Without trying too hard, I bet you can think of a few situations where you've heard a customer saying something to the effect of, "Oh, I didn't know I was supposed to do that." All the while we were thinking, "Of course you have to do that."

Whose fault was that? Yep, that falls right on us. If it's so routine that we expect everybody to know it, shouldn't we take the time to talk about it?

Let's look to my independent adjuster friends for a real life example of what we're talking about. As an independent adjuster, you have a couple of customers

---

[5] "Facts and Statistics: Auto insurance," Insurance Information Institute, accessed August 18, 2021, *https://www.iii.org/fact-statistic/facts-statistics-auto-insurance.*

[6] "Facts and Statistics: Homeowners and renters Insurance," Insurance Information Institute, accessed August 18, 2021, *https://www.iii.org/fact-statistic/facts-statistics-homeowners-and-renters-insurance*

at play here since you're working with the actual customer that filed a claim, but also because you handle claims for an adjusting firm and that adjusting firm works with a carrier. There are likely to be a few gaps in communication here, aren't there?

In these scenarios, one thing we can anticipate is the review and approval process of your report and estimate. Because you work with this firm and this carrier on a regular basis you know the time frames involved for how long it takes to get from your submission to the time it actually reaches the customer's hand.

So does it make sense to tell the customer, "I'm going back to the office to write your report and it will be sent to you after that"? Or can we tweak that message a bit and say, "We want to make sure you have the most accurate report and estimate, so after I write them, they will be submitted for Carrier X to review and add any information from their end, and then they'll provide it to you so you get the complete picture of everything"?

This transparency in the process will give your customer a better understanding of what to expect so that we can avoid misunderstandings in the future.

Now some of you adjusting rockstars may be looking at that second statement in the example and are thinking, "Hey John, that statement is missing a critical component." You've got that right. That's why we're jumping over to the next vowel: "E" for Expectation!

E - Expectation

If you're not setting the expectations of your customers, your customers will. And if they're setting their expectations, you have zero control in meeting them. Of all the Vowels of Claims Experience we'll talk about, I believe expectation setting is the most powerful. The difference between not setting and setting expectations is going from no control to full control.

To really nail down this point, let's go back to Carl Van as he writes, "Awesome Adjusters understand that great customer service is meeting or exceeding customers' expectations and having the talent and the skill to set those expectations. That way they can make sure they exceed them."[7]

You can impact the way the claim will progress, even the way it will resolve, from the way you begin the discussion on day one.

We have to make sure we are setting attainable and reasonable expectations from the first notice of loss all the way through to resolution. Both "attainable" and "reasonable" are key.

First, let's hit on "attainable". If you're not able to meet a certain expectation, you shouldn't be setting it. Even

---

[7] Van, *8 Characteristics*, 113.

if it may sound impressive to your customer, that's only going to dig you into a hole you won't be able to climb out of. Yes, they'll be impressed to hear something that sounds too good to be true (because it is), but the disappointment and let down on the back end will be that much worse than if you just led with reality.

Next, we have "reasonable." Just because you know that a certain task will never, even on the worst of days, end up in a certain situation, that should not be the bar. Just because you've never had an estimate out to a customer in more than 10 days, you shouldn't be setting the bar at two weeks.

Giving a really far out "due by" date that you can easily beat, for example, can leave your customers unsettled and feeling like they're not important to you or that you're even helping them. You may create anxiety for them that they're going to have to live with this problem for a much longer time. Remember, this customer may have a hole in their roof, an undrivable car in the driveway, or bills they've paid out of pocket. Any time in additional perceived delays may hurt this experience that much further.

It's the balanced combination of attainable and reasonable that will set you up for success and will provide your customer with a great experience. If set properly, the fact that you meet the expectation will be a win, but if you exceed an expectation that is reasonable in the customer's eyes, you'll have customers praising you to your companies.

Let's go back to the example we talked about in "anticipation."

If you recall, we were letting our customer know about when they can expect an estimate after we've written it, but it has to go through both the adjusting firm review process and the carrier review process. We ended that section with the following comment, "We want to make sure you have the most accurate report and estimate, so after I write them, they will be submitted for Carrier X to review and add any information from their end, and then they'll provide it to you so you get the complete picture of everything."

Sure, it's great to show transparency in the process, but there are a lot of vague comments in there. What exactly does it mean when we say "after I write" or "once it passes." Another big component of expectation setting is being specific so that there is no room for misinterpretation (read: gray areas). Misinterpretation leads to unhappy customers and we need to be specific and clear so as to avoid these situations.

Why don't we go back and tweak that statement based on our previous experience with our adjusting firm and the assigning company.

"We want to make sure you have the most accurate report and estimate, so after I write them tonight, they will be submitted within 24 hours for Carrier X to review and add any information from their end, and then they'll provide it to you so you get the complete picture of everything, which usually happens within 48 hours. So you should get a response in the next three days."

Sounds pretty good, right? No gray areas. No misunderstandings.

But we've now set the bar for us, our adjusting firm and the company. I want to be clear. It can be a very bad thing to set expectations for things out of your control. If you are not familiar with the company adjuster and their typical cycle time to get back to a customer, do not set an expectation for them to meet. Control what you can control. Remember that this company adjuster is a customer of yours as well!

If you are not accurate on both the "attainable" and "reasonable," you are signing your own death sentence!

If some unforeseen issue arises and we, the adjusting firm or the company, can't meet those expectations, we need to be transparent and communicate it. I've personally seen it plenty of times that when you are proactive about potentially missing an upcoming deadline, customers will be more likely to be understanding. They may not be extremely happy that

74

we did not meet the deadline, but they will understand and appreciate the notification.

Conversely, radio silence is probably the easiest way to torpedo a great customer experience. Not knowing what is going on or what is delaying a task is far worse than the delay itself. You may be tempted to avoid facing an unhappy customer, or leave it to hope or chance that, somehow, your original timeline will be met. But avoiding a difficult conversation today will surely lead to an even more difficult one tomorrow.

Make sure you are setting "attainable" and "reasonable" expectations, striving to at least meet or even exceed these expectations, and in the rare instances when you may miss the mark, communicating to the relevant customer proactively, whether that's the individual customer filing the claim, an internal customer at your company, or one at the carrier you may be working with.

Speaking of an individual customer...

I - Individuality

When talking about Anticipation under the vowel "A", we were using our past history of handling thousands and thousands of claims to help us determine the roadmap for a typical claim. But if we lean too heavily on our experience, we can do so to a fault. The amount of claims being handled can test adjusters by making them jump to conclusions or look at a customer as a policy number or a claim number rather than seeing them as the individual that needs their help through this claim.

If we strive to understand the wants, needs and concerns for *this* customer, we will begin to be on the right track.

If you recall, under Anticipation, we talked about the statistics and how this claim that this customer has just filed may be the only claim they've ever had and may ever have in their lifetime. How we handle this claim for this customer can be the sole thing that impacts how they feel about us as adjusters, the claim process, our Claims department, our company, or even the Insurance industry as a whole!

No pressure there, right?!

You may be thinking that the idea of Individuality is contrary to Anticipation, where we were using our past experiences of hundreds or thousands of claims to predict things for our customer. However we can actually use those predictions to customize our approach for *this* customer.

So how will we get to a point where we can tailor individual approaches? We can start with a little tactic that Glenn Snyder, a former co-worker of mine, taught me.

This tactic is to use a reset button. I'm not talking about a physical button like the front of your Nintendo Entertainment System when things are getting tough trying to save the princess. This is a mental reset button that you can push and that will get you back to the beginning of the game.

The secret to this button is using a physical action that symbolizes the end of our interaction with the last customer and moves us on to the next. For Glenn and I, as inside desk adjusters, the physical button was the telephone. Glenn used to say that no matter what happened on that last call, good or bad, when you hang up, it is a switch. That switch turns off the last interaction and when you pick up the next call, that switch turns on the next interaction. We owe it to our customers to provide them a clean slate of ourselves so that we can provide them our best service.

Now, if you are in the field, the phone might not be your button. You may use the car door as your button.

When you get in your car or truck to leave the last inspection and you shut the door, you shut the door on that interaction and when you arrive at the next inspection site, you open the door to that one.

Now that we've pushed the reset button on this customer, let's get to helping them with their individual claim. Remember that this customer most likely never wanted to pay for insurance. They are most likely forced by their government or the market in some way or other to purchase insurance. And even if this customer is in the extremely small minority that wants to buy insurance, they most certainly still do not ever want to use their insurance.

Using their insurance (read: filing a claim) means something bad happened to them, to their property or to one of their loved ones.

When thinking about how best to help a customer, many people may point to the Golden Rule: do unto others as you would have them do unto you.[8]

Sure, it is never a bad thing to treat someone the way you would be treated, but this is Claims. Shouldn't we do better?

Why not aim for the Platinum Rule: treat people as *they* want to be treated. Just because I may want to be treated a certain way when it comes to a claim, that

---

[8] Matt. 7:12 (New International Version).

does not necessarily mean that this customer wants what I want. Remember, we are looking to provide an experience for this individual and not an experience that would be best for us. We need to find out what is important to this customer at this time and at this place.

Pat Kelahan refers to this process as the "CV of CX" or the Curriculum Vitae of Customer Experience. Think of each customer as having their own personal resume of what they've experienced as an insurance customer. The customer doesn't hand this to us at the first notice of loss, so it's on us to uncover it.

We need to take time to prepare our understanding about the customer, their property, their prior losses, etc. Then, in our discussions, we need to ask more questions about the customer's expectations coming into this process as well as what they're looking for and what concerns they may have.

Let's think of a couple of extreme situations involving material damage to vehicles. Vehicle one is a 2020 Mercedes-Benz S-Class Coupe costing into the six figures. Vehicle two is a 1994 Hyundai Excel Hatchback that, if we're being realistic, shouldn't have collision coverage in the first place.

Both claim reports come in with minor bumper damage from a rear-end accident. If we're just going policy to policy, claim to claim, we might get caught in a trap. We may think of that Mercedes as the priority. We need to make sure everything goes right on this claim. We can't have any mistakes. And we may put the Excel on the back-burner because you think it's a beater car.

(Don't worry. I can say that about the Excel. I had one. In teal green, with no radio or air conditioner. And it was nicknamed the Green Hornet. But back to the issue at hand.)

If we didn't hit the reset button between these two claims, we could be looking at it in all the wrong ways. If we did actually get to know more about these customers, about these vehicles, about what they want, we may be led to handle them in completely different ways.

We may learn that the owner of the Mercedes isn't concerned about the claim at all. She has three other vehicles. Her assistant is handling the claim for her and has already told us that she'll be on the road for the next week so the claim is not top-of-mind.

However, the owner of the Excel works two retail jobs and one of the jobs' paychecks is just barely enough to afford the insurance. They don't have the means to get to work other than this vehicle. So not only do they need it repaired, they need it done yesterday. And by the way, this accident was just the icing on the cake as the aunt that gave the customer this vehicle to help them out passed away earlier this month.

Do you think having these back stories might be valuable as you help these customers with their own individual needs? We obviously do not have a crystal ball to learn these background stories when we see an FNOL report, so how can we uncover them?

You can uncover them by hitting the reset button and using The Big Three to uncover what individual responses these customers need.

One last thing I want to touch on while we're on it. There are going to be times when you are overwhelmed with claim volume. It could be a catastrophe situation (CAT) and it seems like you can't keep up. You may be getting close to deadlines or may even be missing some expectations.

Let's be perfectly honest. This customer that you're speaking to doesn't care about the other claims that are piling up for you. I've heard it before and I've said it before. But all we're doing is making an excuse and that doesn't cut it. There is only one thing this customer wants to speak to you about: how to resolve *their* claim.

If we're missing those deadlines or expectations, let's just own up to it.

Own up to it? Looks like we're heading to another Vowel.

O - Ownership

In the world of claims, we deal with all kinds of situations where someone else's actions can put us in an awfully tough spot.

Let's think about the earlier example we used in Anticipation and Expectation. That situation featured an independent adjuster submitting a report and estimate to their firm, which ultimately sends it to the handling adjuster at the insurance company.

There are many points and people involved along this journey that may ultimately impact the customer's experience. For example, a week passes and the customer hasn't received their check or heard from anybody. Now you're getting a call from the customer, who is understandably upset.

The easy thing to do is to check with your firm's system to see that the estimate was submitted to the company three days ago. Then direct the customer to the company adjuster. You might even have a telephone number or email address to share with them. That may be the easy thing to do, but is it the *right* thing to do? Is it the best thing that you can do for this customer?

Remember, the title of this section is the "Vowels of the *Ultimate* Claims Experience." It's certainly not titled, "The Fastest & Easiest Way for an Adjuster to Get

Through a Claim." You're welcome to write that book, but be sure to use the subtitle "How to Lose a Customer in 10 Days."

If we're looking to do what is best for this customer and to ensure they have the ultimate claims experience, we should take a trip with the Super Bowl MVP. Say it with me, "I'm going to Disney World!"

When companies look for shining examples of how to treat customers, an obvious one is Walt Disney Parks & Resorts, "Where Dreams Come True." Companies strive to have loyal fans just like the folks at Disney, and Disney is not afraid to share what they've learned. The Disney Institute helps other organizations by sharing the insights and best practices of Disney Parks.[9]

One of the major philosophies of the Disney Institute is that "it may not be your fault, but it is your problem." This is exactly how we need to shift our mindset. Sure, the reason the customer has just called us about this claim example has nothing to do with our actions. It wasn't our fault. But now that we have them on the line, it is our problem. A problem that we can ultimately solve or at the very least move the customer closer to resolution.

---

[9] The Disney Institute shares insights at their website, *https://www.disneyinstitute.com.*

Let's think of a couple of ways to help this customer, rather than just passing the buck. You could ask to put the customer on hold while you try to call the handling adjuster to find out what has caused the delay, how much longer will it be delayed and when the check will be in the customer's hand. Then we can relay all of that information to the customer. Job done.

Or, if we aren't able to connect, we can take the responsibility to move it closer to resolution. But we again need to set expectations. If all you can guarantee is that you will continue to try to find out about the delay, say that. But let's give them some more concrete answers.

You could say something like, "I'm going to try to get an answer for you by the end of the day. If I don't have a direct answer by then, I'll give you a call back to let you know. And if it gets to that point, I'll escalate the issue to management." Again, in this scenario, we need to keep in mind that the in-house adjuster is our customer as well, so we need to serve both customers. Going right to a Claims supervisor or manager may not be warranted right out of the gate!

One thing about me in my personal life is that I am actually a terrible customer. It's really because of how I feel about Customer Experience and knowing how *I* would treat *me* in the given situation.

That's why I made an Insurance Nerdery video about Ownership as soon as I was able to do so. I ran into an issue when I was flying out to Cincinnati. Yes, there were some flight delays, but that wasn't where my experience was impacted.

It was when my bags didn't make it to my final destination and were left in Washington D.C. that things started to go awry. I spoke to the baggage folks and they told me that they absolutely would deliver my bag to me wherever I wanted it to be delivered.

So far so good, right?

Well, I did have a couple of issues. First, I was staying at an AirBnB, so I didn't have the luxury of a front desk or door man that could accept delivery if I was not available. Second, I was in town for a conference and would be unavailable for most of the day.

Basically, I just needed to know what kind of time frame we were talking about in terms of when the bag would be delivered so I could plan accordingly. The representative was able to tell me that there were two flights my bag could be put on the next morning, arriving at either 11 am or at 4 pm. She also let me know that deliveries are made every two hours after those flights. So, basically, she told me there may be a 12-hour window of when my bag *might* be delivered and she needed an address to put into their system.

I then told her my problem about not knowing which address I should use or where I should meet up with her delivery team. This resulted in a response of, "It isn't my fault and I can't control what the baggage handlers do in D.C."

That was true. This was not her fault and she certainly couldn't control what the folks in D.C. did or would be doing. But this now *was* her problem. I was looking to her to resolve my problem or at the very least bring me closer to resolution. But saying this did not de-escalate the issue and, if anything, it worsened my experience.

She could not solve this problem herself, just like our independent adjuster that has submitted an estimate to the in-house company adjuster. But she could have found a way to bring me closer to resolution. I certainly wasn't expecting her to solve the problem, but just passing the buck and avoiding the situation guaranteed I was not going to have a good experience.

One thing I'd like us all to agree on is to lose the phrase, "That's not my job."

Are we in agreement that moving forward from today, if we're confronted with something that's "not our job," we choke that back, suck it up, and try to find a resolution?

Again, I'm not asking you to directly solve the problem, because it might not be in our power. But let's move to a point where we are getting the customer closer to a solution.

Do what you personally can do to help this customer.

U - Understanding

We've been talking an awful lot about helping people through a terrible situation where something bad has happened to them, their valuable investment(s), a family member, etc.

As we've been discussing, we have to be the ones helping our customers through this trying time. But is that the only thing we're helping them through?

Let's take a total loss fire for example. We may already have some preconceived notions about this loss and how terrible it might be. Maybe even thoughts of, "Wow, it can't get any worse than that." But that may not be the case for this customer. We're all humans. And human lives are pretty damn complicated. This total loss fire might not be the most difficult thing they're going through.

Unfortunately, as adjusters, our first interaction with this customer is most likely going to be a First Notice of Loss report, an inbound call to report the claim, or showing up to the scene for an inspection. We don't have any idea about this individual's back story. In all actuality, their claim could very well be the least of their worries.

So how can we begin to get an idea about this customer's back story so that we're better positioned to help them through the process? We need to get to a point where we understand this customer, their situation and where they are coming from. And more importantly, we need to understand the true root of their problems. That, right there, is the Holy Grail. If we can uncover what the true root of their pain point is, we'll know what we need to do to help resolve it.

So getting back to this total loss fire example and thinking it's the worst thing they're going through. Sure, their home is destroyed. And they'll have to deal with the rebuilding process over the next few months. But if we strive to understand the root cause or the most vital pain-point for this customer, we can better serve them.

Through this extra effort of understanding, we may find out that our customer's elderly mother is in a nursing facility two blocks away. Our customer would visit their mother every single day. And on those days when it was nice out, it would be a nice stroll over to the facility that would act as a bit of decompression for them.

For this customer, not being within walking distance to their mother is now the biggest issue they're facing. And now that we understand that, we may even be able to assist. Typically when these total loss situations occur, we jump into our Additional Living Expenses mindset and start putting together plans right away for a hotel or rental property in the same town to get our customer settled in.

In this case, that's not what would be ideal for this customer. Perhaps we think outside the box a bit and get a trailer rental on the homeowner's property. Because we understood this customer's biggest issue and provided a creative solution to help them through, we have now shown this customer how much we care about them. And we've been saying it all along: we're in this business to help people.

Before we leave "Understanding" there is definitely one thing we need to dive into. Carl Van refers to this thing as a gift. That gift is a snide remark.

Yes, you read that right. A snide remark is a gift and I couldn't agree more with Carl.

It's a gift if we understand where it's coming from and why. If you've been in Claims for any amount of time you've probably received this snide comment, "It's about time!"

You may have just returned a call, or just showed up for an inspection. And you're struck with, "It's about time!"

With that snide remark, we may be back on our heels and in a defensive position. I'll caution you here not to get defensive. The snide comment could put us in a position where we feel the need to respond and defend ourselves. Remember, it's not a competition between the two of you. In fact, you're on the same team and you both have the same goal. To resolve this claim.

So really the first thing we should do with a snide comment is to come to our first understanding. We need to understand that at that moment, we are the target of the customer's frustration. But we are not the root cause of their frustration.

Carl Van gave us some advice when he wrote, "Yes, this person's being really difficult right now, but they are the ones who've been involved in the accident, not me. So the way I can help is to take a little bit more time and be a little bit more patient, and not take on the anger myself."[10]

If we understand that first, we will be on the same team to resolve that frustration, rather than to defend ourselves, because we really don't need to. But that doesn't mean we stop at the snide comment. We should dig into it.

Perhaps we dig in by saying, "I know your time is extremely valuable. I understand we might not be meeting your expectations for how quickly we can get through this process. I want to be able to help you navigate through this process the best I can, so I'd like to know if there are time frames I should be aware of? Were you expecting the inspection to be at another time?"

---

[10] Van, *8 Characteristics,* 135.

We might learn that we're not honoring their time, or that they have an appointment, time crunch, etc. But remember, we're asking these questions to listen and learn from the customer. We are asking questionsto reach an understanding.

How do we get to this understanding? In his book, *The 8 Characteristics of the Awesome Adjuster,* Van speaks of a very powerful tool in our tool belt: Why? That's right, just using that simple word to dive in further will help us gain a better understanding of where they are coming from.

If we dig a bit deeper into that comment we may learn that they are under a time crunch. They may have a planned vacation that is coming up. If we learn this, we can start to come up with solutions to how we can better help them. Do we need to reallocate our time to make sure we get the claim wrapped up or do we need to bring in other resources? Understanding will help us answer our own questions.

To wrap things up, I have to stick with Carl Van. In *8 Characteristics*, he stated that all Claims folks should hold a common truth. He said, "People will accept what you have to say, to the exact degree you demonstrate you know where they are coming from."[11]

---

[11] Van, *8 Characteristics*, 82.

If we follow this truth, we'll actually be making our job easier. If we truly understand what the customer is going through and we show them that we do, they will be more accepting when we're explaining something, requiring something of them, or even breaking some tough news.

Which circles us back to our total loss fire situation doesn't it?

Y - You

In grade school we probably learned that the vowels were A, E, I, O, U and sometimes Y. Well this is going to be changed up a bit for our vowels. Because our vowels always include Y.

That's because the Y is You.

Let's go back to when I was that punk adjuster just starting out. I got the call from the woman whose husband had just passed away right next to her in that horrific car accident. *She* was depending on *me*!?

To help her through the worst experience of her life? That is the kind of power we're talking about.

We are the experts that are helping people navigate the tricky waters of a claim. We walk them through the actual process, the paperwork and forms, repair estimates, invoices, medical bills, and on and on and on. But that's the easy part.

We're also helping them navigate the waters of their life following this situation. How can they manage? How can they get by? How can things ever get back to normal?

Well, that's where You come in.

Because you're again using the Big Three of listening, caring and empathizing, you know what is really needed to actually take the next steps. You know how to assist with completing and submitting forms, teaching about what to expect during the repair process, during the healing process, during the payment process, etc.

But beyond that, you'll be assisting with how to get people back on their feet. You will be there when they need an ear to listen, a shoulder to cry on, and a sounding board to think out loud with.

It may seem like I'm being overly dramatic with this power that you yield. After all, you're just an adjuster processing claims right?

WRONG!

We should not look any further than Ben Parker (you know, Peter's uncle, from *The Amazing Spiderman*) when he said, "With great power comes great responsibility."

Don't let this being a comic book reference lessen the importance for you.

In all seriousness, you wield enormous power at your desk or in the field as an adjuster. You have the authority in your role to pay thousands of dollars with the simple click of a mouse. That is a huge responsibility to uphold not just for your company, but also for your customers and all the other insureds.

In each and every one of your claims, *you* are a difference maker. You are the reason someone will think what they think about the experience, the claim, or even insurance as a whole. Based on that, they will make a decision of whether this was a great experience, a terrible experience, or it was just something where they went through the motions.

Yes, you are what people will think back on when reflecting on what they have gone through. It was already a tough situation for them. Can't we at least strive to make it a great experience?

One thing we need to keep in mind throughout the life of a claim is that every interaction we have with that customer may be our last interaction. So we need to make it count.

I remember writing an update to the entire Claims department of one of the carriers I worked for talking about our Claims Satisfaction Survey results. I ended the update with this line:

> "Remember, every interaction we have with our customer could be our last chance to WOW them!"

Some folks thought it was hyperbole. Others thought it was just a cry to rally the troops. And those that have made a long career in claims knew that it was fact.

That email you're about to type, that call you're about to make, that appointment you're driving up to may be your last chance to impact this person's life. You might not ever get a chance for a do-over.

If we go into each and every interaction with the intent of providing the best experience possible, that could change the game. That interaction could be the sole differentiator. It can go so far as that customer having a sour taste in their mouth about the insurance industry as a whole and knowing they need to change insurance companies ASAP. Or you could have made the experience so good that you just earned your company a customer for life.

Claims Is Not Your Only Role

"You best believe that I'm not gonna wait
'Cause there's gotta be something more"

—Sugarland, "Something More"

Now that we have the Big Three and the Vowels behind us, we can start talking about looking at bent metal, climbing on roofs, reviewing medical records, etc., right?

Have you even read the previous chapters?

There are other resources out there to talk about all the technical aspects of a career in Claims. If you need help looking for the best, reach out to me on LinkedIn. I love connecting people with other folks that I think might be able to help.

In this section, we're not chatting about specific Claims roles that you may be tasked with. I'm talking about the ancillary roles you are providing the company by just doing your day-to-day tasks - but doing them in a way that can really make a difference.

I remember sitting in company-wide business meetings feeling like one of the unfortunate souls that resided on Claims Island. For those of you not familiar with these all-employee meetings, let me set the stage.

The entire company comes together for a once, twice, maybe even four-time-a-year event where the executives give a sort of "State of the Union" for a company. If it helps you, think of a really dialed back version of one of those famous Steve Jobs speeches, minus the release of a game changing technology.

This is where the CEO and other executives share all of the business results over the past quarter or the past year and try to shed light on how the future looks for the next 90, 120, or 365 days.

They go through some pretty high-level metrics like policies in force, written premiums, earned premiums, investment gains, etc. All of the great work the revenue producing departments are doing to bring in the cash.

Then it comes to talking about loss ratios, combined ratios, catastrophic losses, large losses, etc. Basically all of the dollars being sent out the door by the Claims team. It was during these moments when we were hearing about the impact Claims was having on the bottom line. In those years with major catastrophic losses or an atypically-high volume of large losses, it can be pretty uncomfortable in that room when they talk about the company not making a profit or even losing money.

I know I felt like I was on Claims Island in those tough years. But I don't think it was a lonely island because I think everyone in Claims must have felt the same way.

Let's get real here. Claims *is* a cost center for an insurance company. Claims is sending millions upon millions of dollars out the door. That's a fact.

But it doesn't feel good when you're looking up at those pretty slides and realize that you and your department are the reason for a tough year. I can remember sitting in those rooms as an adjuster and a Claims leader feeling like I was costing the company money.

The reason I felt this way is because I had the mindset that Claims was solely a cost center. It was the other teams in the company that were the revenue making machines, not us.

I turned my mindset into an "us versus them" situation. I thought, "If they just brought in more revenue, we'd be doing alright because our role was to pay what we needed to pay, regardless of what was coming in the door. It's their fault, not ours."

In this section, I'm asking you, the reader, to change this mindset. Especially if you're a Claims leader or someone presenting in these company-wide business meetings. Claims is not relegated to just a cost-center. Claims and the Claims team can absolutely generate revenue for our Companies.

Let's chat about how we can see our Claims roles as revenue generators.

Retention Specialist

If we've followed all of the strategies within the Big Three and the Vowels, you'll provide a great experience. And a great experience can be the difference between a customer for life and someone that will be shopping for a new insurance company.

We talked about it earlier. That you are the difference between a great experience, a terrible experience or even an experience that left the customer feeling empty. You could send that customer right to Google to run a search for "The Best Claims Service Insurance Company" to find a replacement for your company or to leave a 5-Star Review praising the work you and your company have done.

What we're talking about is retention: keeping customers around.

Companies often think about marketing, sales, independent agents, etc., as their revenue generating sources. But that's for new business.

Sure, companies always have (and should have) goals for new growth. But I love to chat about retained business for two reasons. First, a company doesn't need as many new customers to continue to grow if you're keeping your current book of business. Second, the math tells us a retained customer is more profitable for a company.

When it comes to the numbers, the experts don't necessarily agree. Some say it costs five times more to obtain a new customer than to keep an existing one.[12] Others say it's seven times more.[13] And still others say up to twenty-five times more.[14]

Whether you want to believe it's 5x or 25x, one thing is definitely not in question: new customer acquisition costs companies more money than customer retention.

Let's talk more about keeping customers around for a while. It may seem like an easy task on paper, but in Claims we're already facing an uphill battle.

In 2014, the consulting firm Accenture reported on the importance of Claims service and why it matters so much.[15] During their research, they asked people that had a claim how likely they would be to switch insurance in the next year. 41% of the people surveyed

---

[12] Khalid Saleh, "Customer Acquisition Vs. Retention Statistics And Trends," Invesp blog, updated November 11, 2020, https://www.invespcro.com/blog/customer-acquisition-retention/.

[13] Team Kapost, "The Cost of Customer Acquisition vs. Customer Retention," Upland Software blog, https://marketeer.kapost.com/customer-acquisition-versus-customer-retention/.

[14] Amy Gallo, "The Value of Keeping the Right Customers," *Harvard Business Review Online*, October 29, 2014, https://hbr.org/2014/10/the-value-of-keeping-the-right-customers.

[15] "The Digital Insurer Claims Customer Survey: Why Claims Service Matters," Accenture Insurance Blog, 2014, https://insuranceblog.accenture.com/wp-content/uploads/2018/07/Accenture-Global-Claims-Customer-Satisfaction-Survey-executive-summary-POV.pdf.

said they were likely (33%) or very likely (8%) to switch insurance providers in the next 12 months!

OK, now you might already be saying, "WOW!" But I haven't even hit the WOW moment yet. Those people said they are basically switching and we haven't said anything about how good, bad or ugly their experience was just yet. They just had a claim. That's it!

Now let's dive in further. 65% said they were switching if they said they were "dissatisfied" or "very dissatisfied" with their claim experience. That makes sense. They had a tough experience and the Claims folks did nothing to change that experience, so they're likely to leave. We can totally understand that.

On the other side of the coin, let's talk about the people that said they were "satisfied" or "very satisfied" with their Claims experience. 39% of these people said they were likely (32%) or very likely (7%) to switch.

Say what!?

Regardless of what we do as Claims people, these customers are "at-risk" of leaving our company! Like I said earlier, we're already facing an uphill battle. We need to stack the deck in our favor to give us the best opportunity to keep each customer.

OK, we are deep in the weeds of statistics here, so let's not stop now!

In 2018, Bain & Company, a global management consulting company, reported on customer loyalty in the insurance industry based on a 2017 survey they conducted.[16] One thing they found was that insurers that concentrate on building loyalty gain as much as 20 percentage points in Net Promoter Score (NPS) over a 3 year period.

If you don't know about NPS, you need to. A while back, I recorded a short video breaking it down. You can check it out by heading over to https://bit.ly/whatisnps.

As you will learn in that video, Fred Reichheld was the creator of NPS. Way back in 2001, Reichheld wrote an article that gives us more insight into this retained customer concept.[17]

He wrote that a 5% increase in retention in the financial services sector (which includes insurance) results in a 25% increase in profit. It's due to the fact that the operating costs to serve retained customers declines over time, that these customers tend to buy more, that they often will pay a premium to continue with their

---

[16] Henrik Naujoks, et al., "Customers Know What They Want. Are Insurers Listening?" Bain & Company, October 10, 2018, https://www.bain.com/insights/customers-know-what-they-want-are-insurers-listening/.

[17] Fred Reichheld, "Prescription for Cutting Costs," (Boston: Bain & Company, 2001).

current company rather than switch to a competitor, and that they will refer other future customers to you.

OK…the statistics lesson is behind us now.

Let's tie it all back together. We are already starting in a tough position, because these folks have already had a claim so they may be looking elsewhere before the end of the year.

If we use the skills we've talked about throughout this book, we start to stack the deck in our favor to make sure we give them an excellent experience. If we focus on that with each and every interaction, maybe, just maybe, we hold onto our customer and drive in more money for our company. And if we really do a great job, we may have earned a customer for life!

See, we can drive in money just like all those other departments at the insurance company like the sales and marketing teams.

Speaking of those teams…

Marketing & Sales Specialist

As I mentioned earlier, sitting through those all-employee company meetings could be pretty uncomfortable, mostly because of the mindset of Claims being a cost center for the company. So we've dug into how Claims folks can hold onto customers to support the top line revenue, but now let's go even further down the proactive side of things.

Claims folks can be an extension of the sales and marketing teams. No really, I'm serious!

Let me introduce you to a friend of mine.

Doug Brod is a guy I love to chat with in our industry. He's such a unique person because not only was he an adjuster and a Claims manager at a carrier well known for their service, but he is currently a senior district sales manager. If you're new to the industry, this role may also be called an agency manager at other companies, but basically he meets with agents to talk about why the agents should write more business with his company.

So is Doug focusing on price and products when he goes out on these visits? Nope. He even jokes that insurance companies used to sell a piece of paper with a promise on it, but nowadays they don't even sell the paper due to using e-forms. It's just a promise floating out there now!

The most important thing that Doug points to in his day-to-day role that he does is selling the Claims people. When one of the agent's clients has a loss and needs to file a Claim, the Claims people will be there to help the clients through this tough time. And because he lived a life of Claims, he can relay stories in a very unique way to drive home the differences in service at his company from the others.

To make this point a little stronger, let me restate the situation. A senior sales person is using the Claims people to differentiate his company from the rest. The Claims people and the Claims stories are a marketing asset.

The better service you deliver, the better stories the marketing and sales teams have to help them sell more business and ultimately drive in more revenue.

But you're probably thinking, this is still indirect. It's still the sales and marketing folks that are doing those jobs to drive in more business. It's not the Claims team.

So let's dig a little deeper. Earlier I mentioned that claimants should be seen as our customers just as much as an insured or a policy holder.

Let's set up a scenario. You're an auto adjuster that just got a Claim where your insured rear-ended the other party. You take the mindset that this claimant is your customer. That you're going to **listen**, **care**, and

empathize with this customer so that you can **anticipate** their needs. You set proper **expectations** and after setting them, you meet or exceed them. You give this customer an **individual** experience that meets their needs to show how much you care specifically about them. When issues arise you take **ownership**, solving the problems that you can. Even when you personally can't solve the problem, you take the steps necessary to get the customer closer to their problem being resolved. You **understand** their desires and needs throughout their claim because you've been taking cues from them the entire time. **You** have provided the Ultimate Claims Experience.

This claimant will start to think about how well you've treated them as if they were your customer. Then they will think about how their insurance company only interacted with them by sending them premium invoices. When they called about their claim, their company said, "It sounds like it's the other person's fault, you should file through their insurance."

If that's me in that claimant's shoes, and I start having these feelings about how some "random" company is treating me better than my company is, odds are my company isn't going to be my company too much longer.

They may even say right in the midst of the claim, "How do I get a quote from your company?" They may cancel their policy and jump ship right there and then.

They did this because of what you have done for them; because of how you made them feel. And just because they may not ask for a quote right then and there, doesn't mean it's over.

When it's time for their renewal and their company still hasn't treated them the way you have and all they see is the policy renewal and how much premium they'll be paying next year, you better believe they'll be looking for your company's information.

Either way, you have just brought in a new policy to your company. Who says Claims can't be a revenue generating department?

Managing Stress

"And know you're not the only ship out on the ocean
Save your strength for things that you can change
Forgive the ones you can't
You gotta let 'em go"

—Zac Brown Band, "Let It Go"

Stress is a very real thing when it comes to handling Claims and I'd be remiss if I did not include a section in this book to help adjusters and Claims leaders manage their stress levels. If you want to dig in deep on this subject, I recommend checking out Chris Casaleggio and Chris Stanley's book on the topic, *Burned Out Adjuster's Playbook*. They dig deep into this topic to help manage and possibly alleviate high levels of stress so that adjusters can continue to grow and succeed in their careers.

This chapter is just my small piece to help you. I made it a point during my research for this book to ask everyone I spoke to about how we can do a better job of managing stress levels. I have seen the impact it can have on adjusters and Claims teams.

I, for one, had two adjusters on my teams whose stress impacted them so much physically that they had to leave the profession. Although I worked with both of them on stress management strategies, ultimately their health and wellness were compromised. To this day, I still take this as a failure on my part because I was not able to help them through and ensure that they could prosper in a long career in Claims.

I'm certainly not alone. I heard similar stories during the research process of this book.

Real speak time.

Claims really is not for everyone. There, I said it.

Adjusters are working with customers that have quite possibly just dealt with the worst situation in their lives. Something bad happened to them. That is the *only* reason an adjuster is speaking with a customer.

Claims folks aren't delivering a consumer good that when the customer opens it and begins using it, it brings a smile to their face. We deliver service when a customer suffers; when their property has been damaged; when a loved one has been injured;when their business suffers a loss.

Even in the best claim scenarios, when the adjuster has provided the Ultimate Claims Experience, that customer still had a bad day at some point along the claim journey.

I even had one Claims leader say that being an adjuster is on the same level as being a debt collector in that the initial conversations most times are extremely stressful for the customer as they're dealing with a process that they certainly do not want to deal with.

They even said that a parking meter attendant may have better days because it's only in the rare instances when someone sees their car getting a parking ticket that they have the ability to confront the attendant.

Claims folks interact with every customer, most times with both insureds and claimants, and don't have the option to run away after putting a ticket under the windshield wiper.

With this comes a lot of negativity, not only from what adjusters are hearing and feeling. They can even take on some of the pain that their customers feel.

If we do not develop strategies for ourselves to deal with the stress, it may take over our days and possibly even cause us to look for another career.

There are three main headings that I've come across for helping to manage stress when handling claims: Health & Wellness, Mindset, and Tactics. For every individual, a different combination of strategies under these headings may work. Some of these strategies won't work. But just like every claim has individual requirements to meet to result in a great experience, every adjuster has individual needs to manage their stress levels.

Health & Wellness
Just like a flight attendant's instructions to put on our mask before assisting others, we need to attend to ourselves first when handling claims. We need to take care of our own health and wellness to ensure that we can provide the experience our customers deserve.

Pat Kelahan refers to this as self empathy before customer empathy. That we have to understand what we are personally going through in our own lives, so that we can offer up our best selves. There are many things that can help us down this path including diet, exercise, and meditation.

To take it a bit further, for desk adjusters or adjusters working remotely, you need to ensure you're comfortable and be mindful of ergonomics. If you're not sitting in a comfortable spot and you're dealing with stressful situations, this could only exacerbate your stress level.

It may seem crazy, but your diet, level of exercise, and amount of sleep can also help or hinder your stress levels. If you've ever been deployed on CAT duty you know it sometimes feels like there isn't time to eat, never mind getting in time to walk on a treadmill. So this means we typically hit a drive-thru at some point in our day, work through the night and don't exercise. And our way to cope with the stressful day we had on the road may result in alcohol consumption at night to wind down. This just ends up being a band-aid for the short term.

If we eat better, get in a short walk, get a good night's sleep, and limit our alcohol intake, we'll be better prepared to help our customers the next day.

Remembering also that having fun, laughing, and a level of levity with our co-workers can go a long way toward improving how we feel about ourselves and our careers. Ultimately this impacts our mental well being.

Mindset

Perspective in how you approach your career can have a lasting impact on your stress level. If we think of an adjusting career as transactional, as tasks that need to be done to resolve a claim, we've already lost. A career in Claims is a career in service; a career in helping others.

If you go into each day believing that you are the hero that comes in to save the day, to help customers through difficult times, you will understand your purpose. And this purpose is much deeper than tasks and transactions.

It's human nature that during the course of our day, if we experience three good things and one bad thing, we dwell on the one bad thing. It can dominate our mind. We have to proactively emphasize the good that we are doing.

And sometimes it may not be easy. We may have to look for the opportunities where we can help, or even to see any good in a situation. Paraphrasing an old saying that is often attributed to Thomas Edison plainly states it for us, "Opportunity is missed by most people because it is dressed in overalls and looks like work."

But it is critical for us to put in that work, to understand what our impact truly is on our customers.

If we have this mindset of what our role is as a customer servant as opposed to a claim processor or claim taskmaster, we can appreciate the good we do for our customers. And that will outweigh the bad.

Tactics
There are a number of steps to take and processes to implement to set yourself up for success in both your claim handling and management of stress levels. These are just a few that I pulled from interviews with Claims leaders around the country during the research for this book.

First, you need to control your day. Be proactive in everything you do so your day doesn't control you. We all know that unexpected events pop up every day in the life of an adjuster, so if we just react to our day, we lose control. The best way to do this is to work from your activities, diary dates, milestones, tasks…whatever it is that your company calls them.

To be honest, early career John could have really used this advice. My thought was always that if I worked from my inboxes and voicemail that I'd always be on top of the "problem" claims and that it would eventually manage my daily milestones.

Well, I always had a series of expired milestones for the quiet customers. Meaning they were ticking time bombs. Sure, they were not calling me every day or sending me emails, but they weren't hearing from me. The unknown can do many things to a customer's mind, and it will only be a matter of time before they escalate, ultimately adding to our stress levels.

This proactive approach to desk management also allows for those unforeseen events popping up to be handled without a total derailment of your day. Another approach to avoid those derailments is to block schedule.

Block scheduling is when you block off a period of time on your calendar daily or weekly to work on one type of task. Meaning I have a calendar appointment at 9 to 10 to address as many daily milestones as possible, then I may have a 10 to 10:30 block to check my inbox to see if there are any escalated messages that need to be addressed as a priority. This may not always be easy depending on your company processes due to the need for phone coverage, for example. But even in these instances, you may know that phone calls don't normally pick up until 11, so you can set aside time before 11 to address writing and sending letters. The important thing about block scheduling is to avoid distractions from other tasks and to focus on the task at hand.

If you've handled a Claims desk for any amount of time, you know you may have a handful of claims that need extra attention, like ones with upset customers or even attorneys or public adjusters that have made things a little tough for you. And you come in one morning and know you need to address that claim today. But all too often we think, "It will be easier for me to blast through some early tasks and I'll worry about that tough claim later."

But those claims will always sit in the back of our minds, weighing us down, and will impact us mentally. While we're working on the other claims, that claim may even pop up on us and we will then have to react, putting us on our heels. There is a fantastic book by Brian Tracy called *Eat That Frog!* that is all about taking the most difficult task of your day and doing it first thing. By avoiding procrastination, you actually take a heavy burden off of yourself and you can even find satisfaction because the worst is behind you. If you have one of those claims, tackle it first thing and you will definitely lighten your load.

We also have to set realistic expectations for ourselves. You might be able to inspect eight properties and write eight estimates in one day given the ideal situations. But like we said earlier, things pop up and a claim may take longer than usual leaving you time to inspect only four properties. That is why your day needs to be set up in a way for you to succeed.

On the desk side of things, there may be some limitations or hurdles. For example, claims management systems tend not to have "smart" diary systems that let you know how many tasks you have on a given day or even recognize weekends or holidays.

These technologies may allow us to blindly set milestones for ourselves. We know we need to follow up on this claim in 10 days, but that 10th day may already have 15 milestones scheduled, and the ideal load is 12. You've now put yourself even further behind the 8-ball. But we can't let technology be a hindrance or a hurdle. If your claim management system isn't "smart" enough to recognize the number of milestones, holidays or weekends, then use a paper calendar. Seriously! I've seen some adjusters that were the best in managing their desks actually use paper calendars to make tick-sheets for how many milestones they have scheduled. And no, this wasn't back in the carbon-paper or paper file days. This was just a couple of years ago by adjusters that recognized that their technology wasn't enough and made adjustments to ensure success.

Sometimes we may think that company policies or procedures are meant solely for management and do nothing for the front line workers. So as adjusters we may get "creative" to circumvent processes in hopes of easing things. The claims processes are put in place not only for management, but really to help the adjusters as well. Stay disciplined to the approach. These processes may seem to add a step or two onto the front end of a claim, but in all actuality they remove time and trouble on the back end. Think of this as an investment that will pay dividends over time.

For example, perhaps you have a rule of picking up the phone regardless of the task you are currently working on. This may be a pain because you could be in the middle of writing a letter and you don't want to get side tracked. If you don't stop for that call, then that customer leaves a voicemail. Once you finish your letter you check the voicemail and decide to call right back. Now they're not available, so you get their voicemail and you leave a message. You jump into another file and start reviewing medical records. Phone rings. You don't want to get side tracked, so off to voicemail it goes. This cycle can go on and on, as it has for me and many others in the past. When you finally get a hold of the customer, they tell you they wanted to make sure you received the estimate they just emailed you. A call of less than two minutes. A call that in reality wouldn't have completely derailed the letter you were initially writing. But because of the dreaded phone tag, you could have wasted 10, 15, or 20 minutes of calling back and forth. I'm sure an additional 20 minutes in your day could go a long way, and that's just one claim with a little phone tag.

Finally, we have to remember we are humans. We are hearing a lot of negativity throughout our days. We are taking a lot of this negativity on ourselves, whether we notice it or not. Dr. Ray Shelton of the National Center for Crisis Management and the American Academy of Experts in Traumatic Stress refers to Claims adjusters as non-typical first responders. It might be hard to wrap our heads around that because we're not police, fire or EMT personnel, but we act a lot like them. We show up after a traumatic event and we are there to help the individual through the trauma. During this process, we take on the trauma and negativity, and in CAT events we may do it 15 times per day.

Knowing this, we have to be realistic about our well being and our mental health. There are times when we will have a tough claim or a tough call. Typically, once you hang up the phone or go to a new loss site, you're supposed to hit the reset button to give the next customer an individual experience that wows them.

Can we always do that? No, not always.

We need to be able to walk away from a tough situation and take time for ourselves to decompress. Maybe even to vent our own frustration or negative feelings. We owe that to ourselves and to our mental well being as well as to our next customer.

We all need people to talk to. There are people that will listen. Even if you don't think you have an ear at your company or within your circle, people will be there for you. Not to mention I will listen. If you're ever having a tough time or need to vent, hit me up. I'd be happy to listen.

Networking

"You don't owe me a thing
I've been there too
Someone once helped me out
Just the way I'm helping you
If you really wanna pay me back
Here's what you do
Don't let the chain of love end with you"

—Clay Walker, "The Chain of Love"

If you know me at all or have seen me online, it may surprise you that even as late as June 2016 I did not have a LinkedIn profile. Not a weak profile that I didn't really work on or keep up to date, but no profile whatsoever.

At this point in my career, I had worked for the same carrier for 14 years. During this time the employee count fluctuated anywhere between 400 and 500 employees. I made it a point to, at the very least, "know" a good percentage of all of the employees. I felt that with this amount of interaction I was very well networked in the insurance space. If I needed a different perspective, I had 300 folks that I could bounce things off of.

I also had the incorrect perception that LinkedIn was only valuable to those people that were job hunting. Even though I had managers telling me that wasn't the case, still, in the back of my mind, I thought that if I started to put myself out there on LinkedIn, it would be a negative signal.

What I then learned over the next several months is that the actions I've taken and the actions I haven't are what's made me me.

Fast forward to May 17, 2017. I receive a LinkedIn connection request from a guy that has about 12 designations at the end of his name with this message in the request:

Hi. I run an insurance blog called InsNerds and a podcast called Profiles in Risk. I thought they might be of interest. Also, we just wrote a book "Insuring Tomorrow: Engaging Millennials in the Insurance Industry."

Oh great, somebody is trying to pitch me to buy his new book. I could have rejected the request at that point. Who knows where I would be at this point in my life. I do know one thing: because I accepted the connection request from Tony Cañas on that day, my life went into a whirlwind of opportunities. This is not an exaggeration in the least. Let's keep going if you're doubting.

From that connection, I ended up writing an article for Tony and his blog *InsNerds.com* and it was actually the first time I used the phrase "Claims Is The Place To Be."

From there, Nick Lamparelli, who ran the Insurance Nerds podcast *Profiles in Risk* at the time, read the article and noticed that I live in the same town as his mother. He may have also liked the message I was spreading, but I think the connection to Haverhill, Massachusetts was the bigger driver. This started a relationship with Nick that resulted in my first appearance on *Profiles*.

After that appearance with Nick, we got to speaking about other podcasts and we dug into the Agency Nation podcast with the trifecta of Ryan Hanley, Joey Giangola & Sydney Roe. I listened to the next episode and Hanley just happened to be interviewing Nick Ayers and they were chatting about Hanley crashing his drone. I said "what the hell" and decided to send a LinkedIn request to Hanley and mentioned the episode. He accepted not five minutes later and sent me a link to a video about it. A few months later, Hanley mentioned me in front of a room of 700 agents at the Agency Nation Elevate conference after my family and I drove the 10 hours to the conference after my flight was cancelled. I still think I was the only Claims person at the conference!

Hanley also got me hooked up with the 5 AM Club and some amazing people on the independent agency side of insurance. As a good number of these folks were "doing video", next thing you know I'm trying my hand at it. This directly led to me teaming up with Amber Wuollet with our weekly insurance vlog, *The Insurance Nerdery*.

Before I get ahead of myself, let's get back to Nick Lamparelli's podcast. What we discovered through our friendship is that there were some folks in the insurance world all with a BIG similarity. There was a group of us that all lost over 100 pounds at some point or throughout our lives. Get it? BIG similarity! So Nick wanted to set up a podcast with a few of us.

But when I heard Joey Giangola and Bryan Falchuk were involved, I wanted to back out. Hell, Joey lost 100 pounds and got up at 5 AM every morning to work out. Bryan ran marathons, moved to a vegan diet, and even wrote a book called *Do A Day* talking about strategies to take control of your life. I did not belong in this crowd! I lost 70 pounds twice and that's because I yo-yo'ed a couple of times. I decided to do it anyway. What did I have to lose other than my pride and self esteem?

Well, that connection to Bryan ended up developing from an acquaintance relationship into a friendship. So when Bryan was asked to chair a portion of a conference in Chicago and had a schedule conflict, he thought to recommend me. Next thing you know I was moderating a number of speaker panels and on one of those panels was Caleb Stanton of *SocialSurvey*. Shortly after this conference I joined Caleb and worked side-by-side with him on the Insurance team there.

Last but certainly not least, was the Insurance Nerds connection between me and Chris Stanley, founder of IA Path. Another friend that is changing the way things are done in the insurance industry. He even got me to co-author two books with him, *Adjuster's Resume Playbook* and *Insurance Company Adjuster's Playbook*. And Chris is a major factor in this book being in your hands.

Remember I mentioned it wasn't an exaggeration about the whirlwind of opportunities?

I went on and on with those connections to drive home a point. These connections and your network make you who you are. And not connecting or networking can very well keep you where you are and not open doors for you.

If I didn't send the connection request to Hanley, would I have ever been as connected with the agency side of the industry as I am today? I don't know, but I'm pretty positive he wouldn't have mentioned me at the Elevate Conference.

If I let my nerves and self doubt get to me and decide not to do the weight loss podcast, would I have developed a friendship with Bryan? I don't know, but I'm pretty positive he wouldn't have recommended me to the conference organizers.

What I recommend to you is to connect with people. Connect with people outside of your organization. Connect with people out of your city, state and region. But I say all of this with a word of caution.

Do not connect with people with the thought of what they can possibly do for you.

Connect with people with the initial thought of what you might be able to offer them. Ryan Hanley refers to it as "giving without expectation of reciprocation." And, sure, you may be reading this book early in your career and might think, "What could I possibly give to this person?" The answer might be: nothing. And that's okay.

But when I discussed this topic with Chris Stanley, he disagreed with my thinking that you might not be in a position to offer something. For example, if I was a new adjuster looking to connect with Chris, purely thanking him for a recent post, podcast, article, book, etc., that is a gift to Chris. You are giving him support and you may even be giving his posts a boost with a like or a share.

When I reached out to Hanley, I didn't believe I had anything to offer him. Here is the exact message I sent him:

> Late to the game in finding your podcast, but wrapped up listening to the "How to Hire the Agent You Need" episode this morning and loved it. I had to reach out and connect.
> Thanks for doing what you do!
> —John

I was just being authentic with him. I believe this is the key when connecting on LinkedIn.

And an important component to this key is to actually send the message when looking to connect. All too often I see people using the "connect" button on LinkedIn and that's it. How can you be authentic in your request for a connection if all you do is click a button.

Make it a point on EVERY connection request you make, to include a short note.

And include a reason as to why you would like to connect with them. As I mentioned above, it could be as little as "I've seen your posts previously and they've really gotten me to think so I'd love to connect to learn more from your content."

And with all of these new connections you'll be learning, thinking about things in a different way than you might have previously, and it might even open a door to an opportunity for yourself.

I'd love to connect with you and hear what you thought of this book and the concepts. I can't wait to see what your note requesting the LinkedIn connection says!

So with that I'd like to thank you for taking the time to read through this book and I'd appreciate you leaving a review of the book at IAPath.com/successfulreview/. Knowing that you've made it this far really means the world to me. I never would have thought that anyone would be reading words that I've written when I was shaking hands accepting that first adjuster role.

Acknowledgments

Without the following people, this book would not be in your hands. I owe them all a huge debt of gratitude for their time and thoughts. I consider each one a thought leader in their own right, but more importantly I see them as friends.

Chris Stanley, Founder of IA Path and my publisher
Bryan Falchuk, Founder & Managing Partner of Insurance Evolution Partners and my editor
Doug Brod, Sr. District Sales Manager/Former Claims Supervisor and Manager
Chris Casaleggio, Author of *Burned Out Adjuster's Playbook*
Alex Clay, Claims Leader
Pat Kelahan, the Insurance Elephant, Building Consultant for H2M Architects + Engineers
Eric Lindbloom, Claims Leader
Phillip Morris, Vice President, Sales & Marketing for Eberl Claims Service
Lori Pon, Director - Claim Strategy & Innovation
Troy Stewart, President & COO of Brush Country Claims
Carl Van, President & CEO of International Insurance Institute, Inc.

Additional Thanks

The following people have taught me, coached me, inspired me, pushed me. I am not the person I am today without these people in my life and I just want to say thanks.

Tony Cañas, Carly Burnham, Rob Galbraith, Nick Lamparelli, Amber Wuollet & the rest of the Insurance Nerds Community
Ryan Hanley & the entire The 5 AM Club #5amclubins
The IA Path Community
Chris Paradiso
Woody Brown
Bob Lessard
Dave Nelson
Ryan Lawlor
Mike McDonnell
Glenn Snyder
Evan Purmort
Rich Nouza

Other Books for Adjusters by IA Path

- Independent Adjuster's Playbook
- Auto Adjuster's Playbook
- Networking Adjuster's Playbook
- Audatex Adjuster's Playbook
- Hail Adjuster's Playbook
- Adjuster's Resume Playbook
- Insurance Company Adjuster's Playbook
- Burned Out Adjuster's Playbook
- PDR Technician's Insurance Playbook

Made in United States
Orlando, FL
01 November 2022

24109393R00078